IMAGES
of England

EDGBASTON

The Rock Garden, Cannon Hill Park, *c*. 1930.

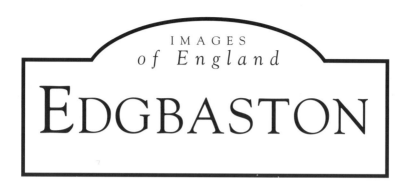

IMAGES
of England

EDGBASTON

Compiled by
Martin Hampson

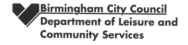

Birmingham City Council
Department of Leisure and
Community Services

TEMPUS

First published 1999
Copyright © Martin Hampson, 1999

Tempus Publishing Limited
The Mill, Brimscombe Port,
Stroud, Gloucestershire, GL5 2QG

ISBN 0 7524 1810 6

Typesetting and origination by
Tempus Publishing Limited
Printed in Great Britain by
Midway Clark Printing, Wiltshire

The cottage garden at Edgbaston Mill, on Edgbaston Lane, 1898.

Contents

Acknowledgements

My thanks are due to Birmingham Library Services (Local Studies, History and Archives) for allowing me to use their photographs. Special thanks are due to Birmingham Botanical Gardens for permission to use pictures on pages 111a, 112b, 113 and 116; and also to John Whybrow Ltd for page 127.

Thanks are also due to Martin Flynn for providing the opportunity to work on this project and for negotiating with the publishers; to Peter Drake for helpful advice; and to Local Studies staff for welcome technical assistance.

Beside Edgbaston Reservoir in 1972.

Introduction

Edgbaston, one of Birmingham's medieval villages, appears in the *Domesday Book* as 'Celboldestone', being owned by William Fitz-Ansculf as a gift from William the Conqueror. Although a manor house and adjacent church were established by the fifteenth century, the village never had a clearly defined centre; Sparry's map of 1718 shows a scattered hamlet with sixty-four houses linked by winding country lanes. For 300 years the lords of the manor were the Middlemores, who were Catholics. Both church and hall were badly damaged by Parliamentary troops during the Civil War, and the hall was totally destroyed by Puritans in 1688 to prevent its use as a Papist base. Following the extinction of the Middlemore male line in 1717, the lordship of Edgbaston was purchased by Sir Richard Gough, a wealthy Welsh merchant, who rebuilt both church and hall and enclosed the park. His son Henry married Barbara Calthorpe, heiress to several estates; his grandson (also Henry) eventually inherited the estates of both parents, becoming Sir Henry Gough-Calthorpe and ultimately Lord Calthorpe.

No member of the Gough-Calthorpe family has occupied Edgbaston Hall since 1783; however, like the Cadburys in the later Bournville, the family has exercised an influence on the character and development of the area that remains all-pervasive. The foundations of this early garden suburb were laid in the late eighteenth century when the first Lord Calthorpe allowed the cutting of the Worcester and Birmingham Canal through his estate on the strict understanding that there were to be no accompanying factories and warehouses; similar restrictions applied to the subsequent West Suburban Railway (later the Bristol main line). It was from about 1810 that the Calthorpe family began to develop Edgbaston as a residential area for Birmingham's more prosperous businessmen, who had previously lived close to their workshops and factories but now sought a greener yet still convenient environment. Much of the farmland now requisitioned for building purposes was little more than a mile from the city centre.

Throughout the nineteenth century, expansion was steady and continuous, initially to the south and west of Five Ways and along the principal access routes to Birmingham. The lines of many old country lanes were followed in the building of the estate; but many new roads were also cut, most of them named after various members of the Calthorpe family or places associated with them. While the main emphasis was on fairly large detached or semi-detached houses, some good quality working-class homes were also built in the area bordering on Ladywood and Lee Bank. Ninety-nine-year building leases were created, with restrictive covenants to allow residential development only. A number of very large houses with extensive grounds (around $2\frac{1}{2}$ acres) were built as the century advanced – a sign of increasing affluence. The population rose steadily, from 3,954 in 1831, to 9,269 in 1851, to 22,760 in 1881. Edgbaston became part of Birmingham in 1838.

By the 1880s, the basic street pattern was completed, half of the estate consisting of low-density housing, and half of open space (mainly farmland, but also private parks and gardens, nurseries, sports grounds and building plots). From the beginning, the Calthorpe family encouraged the development of educational establishments – special institutions for the deaf and blind, as well as more conventional schools, and later the Teacher Training College and University. Organizations of a conservationist and educational nature like the Botanical Gardens were also encouraged, as were spacious venues for such sports as archery, croquet, tennis and cricket. The predominance of Anglican churches reflected the Calthorpes' own religious leanings. New public houses were discouraged, though some existing ones were allowed to remain. No shops were permitted on residential roads until 1918, and there was strict control over tree-felling, even on private land. In the 1930s, the

Head Forester estimated there were at least $1\frac{1}{4}$ million trees on the estate, encompassing 172 varieties, many nearly 300 years old and up to thirty feet in girth. The establishment of the community magazine *Edgbastonia* in 1881 confirmed the close-knit character of the area.

By the end of the century, three clearly defined local architectural styles were apparent – stuccoed white Georgian, redbrick Gothic, and Arts and Crafts. Many Edgbaston mansions were the urban equivalent of country houses, social and political meeting places for the local ruling class. The leading families were mainly Nonconformist and Liberal in persuasion, the dominant group being the tightly-knit, inter-related Unitarians.

Between the wars, although Edgbaston's residential character remained largely unchanged, the southern part of the estate was developed increasingly for institutional use. The Queen Elizabeth Hospital and the King Edward's Schools (transferred from New Street) were built adjacent to the expanding University site, while near the Harborne boundary the Blue Coat School (transferred from Colmore Row) and the Harborne Hill School were also erected.

By the 1950s, the larger Victorian mansions – difficult to maintain without adequate staffing – were becoming neglected, empty or subject to rough conversion to flats and offices. Birmingham by now had little room for outward expansion, and the report by local architect John Madin in 1958 recommended increased housing density in Edgbaston and commercial development at Five Ways to relieve city-centre office congestion. The leasehold system allowed the acquisition of land without compulsory purchase orders being needed by the council, and by the late 1950s many of the original leases were due to expire. Redevelopment was thus implemented in stages during the period 1958 to 1967, particularly in the Augustus Road area, where many of the largest houses had been built in the 1860s. Wherever possible, the new smaller houses and flats were erected within the original mature Victorian gardens, thus retaining much of the green and spacious character of the estate.

The implementation of the Madin Plan created a more mixed and varied area without sacrificing essential character. Some high-rise flats were permitted, and some council housing following the sale of land on the Lee Bank/Pershore Road side. Five Ways has been developed as a major commercial area, with two new shopping precincts and a large office quarter (modern high-rise blocks and older house conversions), and three further shopping centres have been built elsewhere on the estate.

As befits the cradle of lawn tennis and Warwickshire County Cricket, Edgbaston is internationally known in sporting circles. The strong link with education continues, with the University of Birmingham and UCE Faculty of Education continuing to expand. Most of the city's independent schools remain in Edgbaston, and several of its best-known hospitals. The 'green' character of the area is maintained not only by the survival of so many tree-lined roads and wooded private gardens, but also by the remarkable preservation of so many large tracts of open space, most of them publicly accessible. Cannon Hill Park and the Botanical Gardens make important contributions to the semi-rural environment, as in their own way do major sporting venues like Edgbaston Golf Club and the Priory Tennis Club (both grounds remaining remarkably unspoiled), and the University's Vale Halls of Residence site. Whether seen as an early planned suburb, or sought for its fine parks and gardens, or as a centre of excellence in education, healthcare, or sport, Edgbaston can mean different things to different people. This collection of photographs attempts to reflect the variety in older and more modern scenes.

One
Rural Edgbaston

Edgbaston Mill, on Edgbaston Lane, 1898.

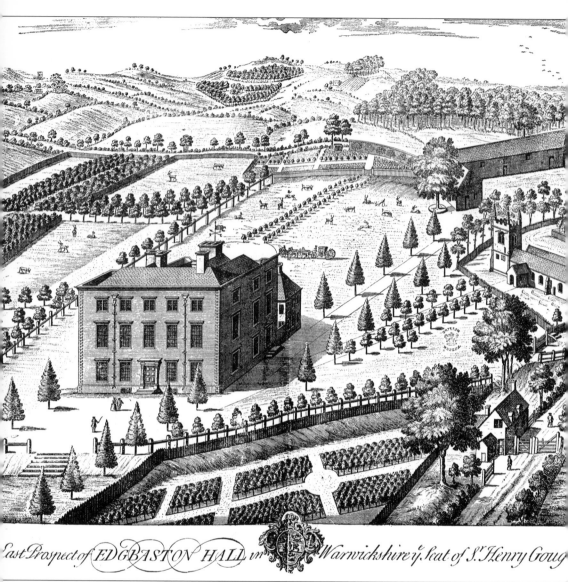

East Prospect of EDGBASTON HALL in Warwickshire ÿ Seat of S.ʳ Henry Goug...

An eighteenth-century prospect of Edgbaston Hall and Park. The original fifteenth-century manor house, the seat of the Middlemore family, was badly damaged during the Civil War, when it was seized and garrisoned by Parliamentary troops, and was burned down by local Puritans in 1688. The present building dates from 1717, when Sir Richard Gough, who had purchased the estate from the Middlemores, rebuilt both church and hall and enclosed the park. His son Henry married Barbara Calthorpe, heiress to several estates, their son (also Henry) becoming Sir Henry Gough-Calthorpe and ultimately Lord Calthorpe. No member of the Calthorpe family lived at the house after 1783, and it was let to a succession of tenants, of whom William Withering, who discovered digitalis, is probably the best known. The hall narrowly escaped destruction in July 1791 at the hands of 'Church and King' rioters because Dr Withering was a member of the Lunar Society, which was noted for its advanced religious and political views. Although the engraving shows a traditional manorial setting of church and hall, Edgbaston never had a distinct village centre, being until its nineteenth-century suburban development a widely scattered rural hamlet.

An early nineteenth-century engraving (*c.* 1829) of Edgbaston Hall, showing the landscaped grounds laid out by Capability Brown. The park retains much of its original character, having been leased since 1936 to Edgbaston Golf Club.

Edgbaston Pool, below the hall, *c.* 1890. This was originally the manorial fishpond and is now an important wildlife site; 130 species of bird have been recorded here.

Over Mill on Chad Brook, *c.* 1900. Just south of Edgbaston Pool in Edgbaston Park, this was once a blade-mill. Other mills in the district were Edgbaston Mill and Speedwell Mill on the Rea, and Pebble Mill on the Bourn Brook.

Seventeenth-century estate cottages on Ampton Road, converted from a farmhouse, seen here around 1960.

The White Swan and village pound on Harborne Road, *c.* 1890. The pound, which was used to confine stray animals, had previously stood on Hagley Road, and before that near the entrance to Edgbaston Hall.

Hawthorne Road, opposite the White Swan and adjoining Chad Valley Nurseries, led past some eighteenth-century cottages towards the Victorian mansions of Oak Hill and Berrow Court (later a hotel). Part of the old settlement known as Good Knaves End, it retained a semi-rural atmosphere till the late 1960s, when the area was redeveloped for modern housing; this picture dates from 1968.

An early nineteenth-century cottage on Westfield Road, *c.* 1900.

This farmhouse on Westfield Road, pictured in 1906, was typical of several working farms still to be found in Edgbaston at the turn of the century.

The bridge over the River Rea, on Edgbaston Lane (now Edgbaston Road), close to Cannon Hill Park, 1898. The Rea, built up for much of its course through Birmingham, is seen to greatest advantage in the Cannon Hill area.

Edgbaston Mill, on Edgbaston Lane, 1898. The site of this corn-mill on the River Rea was later occupied by the Tally Ho Tennis Club, the mill house being only recently demolished.

Metchley Park Road, 1933.

Cottages and farm on Rotton Park Road, 1903.

These cottages on Somerset Road – like some other 'rural' houses in Edgbaston – were demolished in the 1960s, shortly after this picture was taken.

Haymaking at another working farm, on Meadow Road, 1909.

Two
Street Scenes and Landmarks

Joseph Sturge's statue and King Edward's Grammar School, Five Ways, *c.* 1895.

Edgbastonia was a monthly community magazine published between 1881 and 1934, 3,000 copies of which were distributed free to householders. Claiming to be the 'only magazine chronicling all the social events of the month' and to be 'free from political or sectarian bias', it featured a wide variety of articles of current local interest, as well as historical and literary studies, and short biographies of local worthies. The cover features five Edgbaston churches – the Church of the Redeemer, St James's, St Augustine's, St Bartholomew's and St George's – while the Gothic arch in its design is a clear reference to one of the characteristic architectural styles of the area.

Looking up Hagley Road from Five Ways around 1905, with the statue of Joseph Sturge on the left and a horse-bus waiting to go down Broad Street into town on the right.

Crossing the road at Five Ways, at the junction of Calthorpe Road and Harborne Road, *c.* 1928. Though medieval Edgbaston lacked a clear focal point, Five Ways has become the modern commercial centre, particularly since the war.

Five Ways, Birmingham.

Looking from Five Ways down Broad Street, c. 1920. Two surviving (though repositioned) landmarks are visible – Joseph Sturge's statue and the clock tower. None of the buildings shown in this photograph now survive.

A closer view of Joseph Sturge's marble statue, c. 1900. Unveiled by Mr W. Middlemore in June 1862 in the presence of 12,000 people, and standing today in front of the Swallow Hotel, it commemorates Joseph Sturge (1793-1859), a Quaker corn merchant who came to Birmingham in 1822. He played a major part in the abolition of slavery and later in the temperance movement.

The clock tower at Five Ways, hung with advertisements for the British Industries Fair at Castle Bromwich, 1955. The Five Ways Inn can be seen to the left, with Broad Street straight ahead and Islington Row to the right. Of the buildings in this picture, only Lloyds Bank (built in 1908/09 by P.B. Chatwin) now survives.

This Georgian town house, built around 1800, stands at the junction of Harborne Road and Calthorpe Road, Five Ways. Like many listed buildings in the area, it has been in recent years successfully converted to office accommodation. It is seen here in 1953.

The now-vanished gardens at Five Ways, looking towards the clock tower, Islington Row, and Lloyds Bank, 1935.

A similar view, taken in 1968, shows the transformation of the 1960s and 1970s already under way. The Five Ways Inn and Lloyds Bank remain, but the shape of things to come is seen by the appearance of Auchinleck House (1964), one of the first large office blocks to be built in the area, with a shopping precinct (Auchinleck Square) beneath it.

A view from Five Ways offices in the 1970s, looking over the Calthorpe Estate towards the University tower (centre background), and showing the still open and wooded character of the residential area, with the recent office developments in the business quarter in the foreground.

Islington Row, just off Five Ways, *c.* 1920. None of the buildings in this picture have survived.

A scene in Calthorpe Road, *c.* 1910.

Charlotte Road, *c.* 1900. Named after Lady Charlotte Somerset, the wife of the fourth Lord Calthorpe, the road was prepared for building between 1830 and 1847, the houses being erected mainly in the 1850s, with occasional building until 1901. 'Substantial' houses cost £500, and smaller ones £300 in this typically well-wooded Edgbaston road.

Roadworks on Hagley Road, at the junction with Norfolk Road and Rotton Park Road, 1923.

HAGLEY RD EDGBASTON

A tram passing down Hagley Road, c. 1920. There was much opposition from local residents to the introduction of trams along this road – they were seen as noisy and downmarket – and the service only lasted from 1913 to 1930.

Hagley Road at the junction with Monument Road, 1891.

The Plough and Harrow Hotel, Hagley Road, seen from Highfield Road, c. 1900. Hagley Road has for many years been noted for its hotels (many of them conversions from large private houses).

The southern end of Monument Road, c. 1900. The 'monument' referred to is Perrott's Folly.

Perrott's Folly, or the Monument, seen from Waterworks Road in 1968. This striking six-storey octagonal tower, 96ft high, was built in 1758 by John Perrott, lord of the manor of Rotton Park, at that time an extensive deer park and hunting ground. It is believed that he used it for entertaining friends and viewing the surrounding countryside.

Above: There is one room on each floor of Perrott's Folly. This view (taken in 1949) shows the characteristic pointed windows and elaborate plaster ceiling.

Left: Perrott's Folly in 1957, showing the full height of the tower. From 1884 it was used as a weather observatory, first by the pioneer meteorologist Abraham Follett Osler, and later by the University of Birmingham. In 1984 it was purchased by the Perrott's Folly Company, and is now open occasionally to the public.

The view from Perrott's Folly in 1913, looking towards Edgbaston Reservoir and Rotton Park Road. Rising to the right is the Venetian Gothic tower of the Pumping Station, designed in 1870 by John Henry Chamberlain. The writer J.R.R. Tolkien lived locally for a time, attending the Oratory School, and these two towers are believed to have suggested Minas Morgul and Minas Tirith, the Two Towers of Gondor, in his fantasy trilogy *Lord of the Rings*.

This ornate Gothic fountain (seen here around 1890), at the junction of Hagley Road and Sandon Road, was a prominent landmark through the late Victorian and Edwardian period.

A closer view of the now demolished fountain, c. 1910.

Cutting Jacey Road, *c.* 1930.

Children in Waterworks Road (Monument Retreat), 1968.

Hall's glass, china and hardware stores, in City Road, *c.* 1900. The Halls had three shops in this area. (Being outside the Calthorpe Estate proper, shops were permitted here, even at this time.)

An open-topped bus on Hagley Road, 1912.

Excavations at Metchley Roman Camp, 1968. Earlier excavations in 1934 and 1954 had revealed the existence of two forts on the site, the earlier and larger one being defended by a double ditch and bank enclosing $14\frac{1}{2}$ acres. The later fort was smaller ($6\frac{1}{4}$ acres), built within the previous one and defended by a single bank and ditch.

The remains of timber buildings found on the site were used as the basis for the reconstructed watch-tower, erected around 1950 to show what the original looked like. Unfortunately, the tower soon succumbed to the attentions of vandals, and it was later demolished and the site landscaped. The cutting of the railway and canal and the building of the Queen Elizabeth Hospital have obliterated much of the fort's original foundations.

An open-topped tram on Bristol Road, *c.* 1905. Although a service of accumulator cars had run from the city centre to Dawlish Road as early as 1890, 'modern' electric tramcars first ran along the Bristol Road in 1901. Initially terminating at Chapel Lane, Selly Oak, the service was extended in 1923 to Longbridge, and in 1924 to Rednal.

A Bristol Road tram running along the central reservation in 1950. The introduction of trams on Bristol Road aroused much less opposition than on Hagley Road because the route ran close to the boundary of the Calthorpe Estate. Between the wars, the route was exceptionally popular with visitors to the Lickey Hills. The tram service lasted until 1952.

Bristol Road in 1895, looking towards the city centre, with the spires of Wycliffe Baptist church and the Unitarian chapel straight ahead.

The same scene in 1954, little changed apart from an increase in traffic. The large houses on the right were replaced in the 1960s by a modern housing estate.

A tram on Pershore Road near Pebble Mill, in 1922. A tram service ran from the city centre to Cotteridge between 1904 and 1952.

The old tollhouse on Pershore Road near Pebble Mill, c. 1930. Pershore Road was cut through in the early nineteenth century. Other tollgates were situated at Five Ways, by the entrance to Edgbaston Hall, at the Hagley Road/Sandon Road junction, and on Bristol Road at Edgbaston Lane.

The junction of Gough Road and Sun Street West, photographed in 1960 shortly before the comprehensive redevelopment of the whole Lee Bank area.

Lee Crescent, 1954. The whole of the left-hand side was later removed in the redevelopment of the area, so that Lee Crescent now looks directly across to the Lee Bank estate.

Bristol Street, looking past the old St Luke's church and Wycliffe chapel towards Bristol Road and Edgbaston, 1895. Bristol Road was cut through to Bournbrook in 1771, replacing the wandering medieval route through Holloway Head, Wheeleys Road, Priory Road, and Edgbaston Park. A tollhouse was erected at the junction with Edgbaston Lane (now Edgbaston Road), and much of Victorian Edgbaston's early development occurred along this route.

The Bell Inn, on the corner of Great Colmore Street and Bristol Street, showing in the background the first flats of the Lee Bank Estate. This is a transitional scene from the early 1960s.

Decaying early Victorian houses on Francis Road, with new flats rising in the background, 1968.

Topping out ceremony at Tricorne House, Five Ways. A modern office block epitomizes post-war commercial development in Edgbaston, 1974.

These modern flats photographed in the 1970s typify the high-quality post-war residential developments which have gradually replaced many of the larger Victorian mansions as their leases expired. The new houses and flats frequently occupy the original mature mansion grounds.

Three
People and Houses

A Georgian-style mansion on Wellington Road, typical of Edgbaston's earliest building phase, seen in 1975.

Edgbaston Hall, 1899. The core of the hall remains the Georgian house of 1717, with the later addition of a two-storeyed north-east wing and some alterations made in 1852 by Sir Charles Barry. It remained a private residence until 1932, the last tenant being Sir James Smith, the first Lord Mayor of Birmingham (in 1896/97). The lease then reverted to the Calthorpe Estate, who in 1936 granted it to Edgbaston Golf Club, when they moved there from Warley. Like several other fine courses (including Wimbledon), Edgbaston Golf Course shares the distinction of having been originally an eighteenth-century park landscaped by Capability Brown.

Wyddrington, on Church Road, as sketched by Allen Everitt in 1858. It was at this time the home of the Mayor of Birmingham, the brassware manufacturer Sir John Ratcliff. The site is now occupied by Birmingham University halls of residence, several of whose names commemorate the former mansions in the area.

Rotton Park Lodge, Rotton Park Road, *c.* 1914. At this time it was the home of James R. Turner JP and the picture shows the carriage of the visiting Lord Mayor.

Edgbaston Grove, adjacent to Wyddrington, took its name from an avenue of beech-trees planted to shelter the hall from north-east winds. This view dates from 1954.

Edgbaston Grove was subsequently demolished, being replaced by the Judges' Lodgings (seen here in the 1980s), which are used by visiting judges attending Birmingham Crown Court. Much of the original garden layout, including the grand entrance, has been retained.

Longworth, on Priory Road, was designed by John Henry Chamberlain for John Thackray Bunce, being completed shortly before Bunce's death in 1899. It is seen here a couple of years later. Subsequently occupied by his daughters Kate and Myra, it now forms part of the Priory Hospital complex.

John Thackray Bunce (1828-1899) edited the *Birmingham Post* for thirty-six years, being a particularly strong champion of educational and cultural causes. A founding father of the Museum and Art Gallery and School of Art, he was also a notable local historian, best remembered today for his history of Birmingham Corporation. His daughter Kate (1856-1927) was a noted Pre-Raphaelite artist who – in addition to some striking mythological paintings – undertook much artwork for churches in collaboration with her sister Myra.

Mariemont on Westbourne Road, *c.* 1900. This house was for some years the home of Sir Oliver Lodge and a favourite meeting place for prominent intellectuals of the day, including Shaw, Bergson and William James. It was demolished in the 1950s, along with several other mansions, to make way for what is now the Faculty of Education of the University of Central England.

Sir Oliver Lodge (1851-1940) was the first Principal of Birmingham University, a scientist whose love of the arts did much to bridge the gap between divided faculties (arts in the city centre, science in Edgbaston). Previously Professor of Physics at Liverpool and the author of several works on electricity, he did pioneering research on x-rays and wireless telegraphy. He was also interested in seeking a synthesis between the paranormal and natural science.

Robert William Dale (1829-1895) was for many years Minister at Carrs Lane church. A keen advocate of the 'civic gospel', he believed that Christian principles should be actively applied to local government. A founder of the National Education League (1869), he was a pioneer of state education, arguing that schooling should be compulsory, free and secular.

Number 115 Bristol Road, seen here in around 1900, was the home of Dr R.W. Dale.

Bishop's Croft (now Queen's Theological College, seen here in 1963), on Somerset Road, was formerly the home of the Rt Revd Charles Gore, first Bishop of Birmingham.

The Rt Revd Charles Gore (1853-1932), while still Bishop of Worcester, became actively involved in establishing the new Birmingham diocese, over which he presided from 1905 to 1911. A liberal theologian, he favoured inter-denominational dialogue and as a Christian Socialist concerned himself with many political and social issues, including housing, temperance, lead poisoning, and wartime atrocities. On his translation to Oxford, a statue was erected outside St Philip's Cathedral in his honour.

Whetstone, at the junction of Farquhar Road and Somerset Road, was designed by the architect John Henry Chamberlain as his own residence, in his characteristic Gothic style. It is seen here at the turn of the twentieth century; it was demolished in the 1960s to make way for Whetstone Close.

John Henry Chamberlain (1831-1883), a keen follower of Ruskin, designed with his partner William Martin a number of elaborate Gothic mansions – many of them in Edgbaston. They were characterized by their ornate tiling and terracotta work, wood-carving and stained glass, and Highbury, in Moseley, is probably the best known. Chamberlain also designed a number of remarkable public buildings, including Birmingham Reference Library and School of Art, several waterworks and baths, and a number of board schools with their characteristic spiky ventilation towers. The entire anteroom from The Grove in Harborne has been preserved in the Victoria and Albert Museum as an example of his richly decorative interior design work.

This house in Calthorpe Road was John Cadbury's home for thirty-five years; his son George was born here on 19 September 1839. It is seen here in 1900.

Although more closely associated with Bournville, George Cadbury (1839-1922) spent his most formative years at the house in Calthorpe Road, Edgbaston, which his father John had bought in 1835. The then semi-rural environment encouraged his lifelong habit of early rising and long walks or horse-rides, and no doubt influenced his planning of the later garden suburb of Bournville. Cadbury's cocoa and chocolate business remained in the city centre, scarcely a mile away, until 1879, when the Bournville factory was founded.

Southfield on Church Road, the home of the Liberal politician Jesse Collings, in 1901. It stood in three acres of land, recalling his famous slogan 'three acres and a cow'. The site is now occupied by Hallfield School.

The library at Southfield in 1901. It contained an ornate Gothic bookcase designed by John Henry Chamberlain.

The drawing room at Southfield, 1901.

Jesse Collings (1831-1920) was the first Mayor of Birmingham to occupy the new Council House (in 1878/79), officially opening the building and hosting the first reception there. A founder of the National Education League (1869), he was a major force in the rebuilding of the Reference Library following its destruction by fire. He subsequently became Liberal MP for Bordesley, making his mark as an agricultural reformer, a champion of allotments and smallholdings.

A rare portrait of the Chamberlain family together in around 1900, with sons Neville (left) and Austin (centre) standing with Joseph, and daughter Beatrice and Joseph's American wife, Mary Endicott, seated. Though Birmingham's best-known political family are more commonly associated with Highbury in Moseley, they also had close connections with Edgbaston. Neville lived for many years at Westbourne, on Westbourne Road, next to the Botanical Gardens (whose car park now partly occupies the site). Joseph and his first wife Harriet lived after their marriage on Harborne Road, where their daughter Beatrice and son Austin were born. After Harriet's sudden death, Joseph lived for some time at Berrow Court, the home of her father, Archibald Kenrick. Joseph's enthusiasm for the house and garden at Berrow Court led to his employing the same architect (John Henry Chamberlain) for the building of Highbury, and influenced his layout of the grounds there, including the construction of an orchid house. Both Joseph and Neville were generous patrons of the Botanical Gardens.

Joseph Gillott (1799-1873) shared with Josiah Mason the credit of having perfected the steel pen. His Victoria Works in Graham Street was a world leader by the 1870s, producing an estimated 14 million nibs a week. He had an estate in Rotton Park (hence today's Gillott Road), and a mansion in Westbourne Road, Edgbaston, where he amassed a notable collection of paintings and violins.

George Dawson (1821-1876) was a noted preacher and lecturer, Minister of the Church of the Saviour in Edward Street ('the church without a creed') and a passionate advocate of religious and political freedom. Another preacher of the 'civic gospel', he was a founding father of Birmingham Reference Library, remarking at the opening of the library in 1865 that 'a great town is a solemn organism, through which should flow, and in which should be shaped, all the highest, loftiest and truest ends of man's intellectual and moral nature'. He lived on Harborne Road, Edgbaston.

Yateley Road has a number of fine 'Arts and Crafts' houses, of which No. 21, designed as his own home by the architect Herbert Tudor Buckland (1869-1951) and seen here in 1902, is among the most stylish.

The dining room of H.T. Buckland's house, 1902.

Winterbourne, on Edgbaston Park Road, in 1985. The house was designed by Joseph Lancaster Ball for the screw manufacturer John Sutton Nettlefold. Completed in 1904, it is a masterpiece of the 'Arts and Crafts' country house style, with its mellow rustic brickwork and wavy roofline. The extensive grounds were laid out by Mrs Nettlefold on the principles of Gertrude Jekyll; they are now the botanical gardens of the University of Birmingham, and the house is its extramural department.

John Sutton Nettlefold (1866-1930) was a screw manufacturer whose family firm ultimately became GKN. The Unitarian families of Nettlefold and Chamberlain were already inter-related through marriage when John Nettlefold married a distant cousin, Margaret Chamberlain; the links were further strengthened by Joseph Chamberlain's having been for some time a partner in the family firm. The Nettlefolds entertained a great deal at Winterbourne, being particularly involved with the Unitarian business and political families – the Beales, Chamberlains, Kenricks and Hopes. J.S. Nettlefold was an active local councillor, interested in housing reform. His most lasting achievement was the creation of the Moorpool Estate in Harborne, a low-cost, low-density garden suburb run on co-ownership principles.

Masshouse Farm, on Pritchatts Road, dates from the late seventeenth century. Following the destruction of the city's Catholic chapel of St Marie Magdalen in 1688, the centre of Catholic worship moved to Edgbaston, then a remote rural area whose manorial family, the Middlemores, were themselves Catholic. Not only were Masses said regularly at the farm, but a Franciscan school was established here in 1723. The very high garden walls (to ensure privacy) were only lowered in 1932. The house ceased to be a Catholic centre following the Catholic Relief Act of 1778 and the consequent opening of St Peter's church and school off Broad Street. It was later owned by the Harrison family (hence Harrison's Road) and survived as a farm into the present century, the last tenant having a considerable milk round. Narrowly escaping demolition in 1932, it has survived as a private residence, as pictured here in 1966, with imaginatively converted outbuildings.

The artist Joseph Southall (1861-1944) at his easel at his home in Charlotte Road. An admirer of Italian Renaissance art, he sought to master the art of painting in tempera, mixing colours with egg yolk and water instead of oil (and keeping chickens to ensure a regular egg supply). He favoured mythical and medieval subjects, but he also handled modern themes, for example in his pacifist studies and in his fresco of Corporation Street in 1914 (displayed on the staircase of Birmingham Art Gallery). As a Quaker, he resolutely opposed the First World War, and followed William Morris as a pioneering socialist.

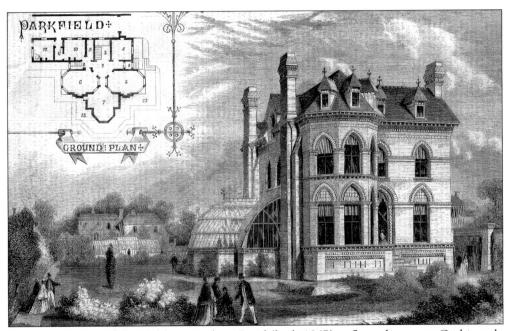

Cranston's design for Parkfield, on Pershore Road (built 1867), reflects the ornate Gothic style favoured by many Edgbastonians.

Garth House on Edgbaston Park Road was built in 1901 by William Henry Bidlake (1861-1938) for Ralph Heaton, then head of the Birmingham Mint. It is seen here shortly after it was built. Now owned by the University of Birmingham, it retains many of the original features of its fine Arts and Crafts interior.

The hall and staircase of Garth House, shortly after completion, 1901.

The drawing room at Garth House, 1901.

Lansdowne, Wellington Road, *c.* 1900. This house was built around 1828 and considerably extended around 1876 for John Henry Shorthouse (1834-1903), a Quaker chemical manufacturer and writer, the author of a popular historical novel, *John Inglesant* (1881). Lansdowne is typical of many white-stuccoed mansions on Wellington Road, one of the earliest roads to be laid out on the Calthorpe Estate and one of the most ambitious, still retaining much of its original character.

South Bank, on Harborne Road, was the home of the glass manufacturer Abraham Follett Osler and is shown here during the 1890s. One of Edgbaston's larger estates, South Bank occupied the whole of the triangle between Vicarage Road, Harborne Road and Westbourne Road – a site now occupied by a number of modern (and still quite large) houses.

The drawing room at South Bank in the 1890s.

Abraham Follett Osler (1808-1903) was a world-famous glass manufacturer, whose Broad Street factory supplied crystal chandeliers to the mansions of the nobility, and whose great crystal fountain was one of the highlights of the Great Exhibition of 1851. He was also an amateur scientist of some note, inventing the anemometer (for measuring wind velocity) and setting up one of the earliest weather observatories on the top of Perrott's Folly. He was keenly interested in electrical inventions, bells and clocks, his most famous gift to the city being the Art Gallery clock, 'Big Brum'.

A fashionable Edgbaston drawing room, 1902.

Four

Churches

St Bartholomew's, Edgbaston Old Church, 1873.

St Bartholomew's, the old parish church, in the early nineteenth century, from a drawing by Charles Radclyffe. Although a small chapel is mentioned as being on this site as early as 1340, the present building was founded in around 1500 by the Middlemore family, then Lords of the Manor of Edgbaston. The church was extensively damaged by Parliamentarian troops during the Civil War, when roof materials were used to barricade the hall, lead from the roof was melted down for bullets, and horses were stabled in the church. Only portions of the nave, north aisle and tower now remain of the original building, which was extensively repaired in the late seventeenth century, and underwent major restoration by J.A. Chatwin in the 1880s.

The funeral of Chief Superintendent Alfred Tozer, member of a famous fire-fighting family and a key figure in the development of the modern Birmingham fire brigade, at St Bartholomew's on 28 April 1906. Other well-known people buried here include William Withering, a founder of the General Hospital and a pioneer in digitalis research, and Gabriel Jean Marie De Lys, founder of the Deaf and Dumb Institution in Edgbaston.

Edgbaston Old Vicarage (now demolished), *c.* 1890.

St George's church, Calthorpe Road, 1873. The original church was built between 1836 and 1838 to designs by J.J. Scoles, on land provided by George, third Lord Calthorpe, and largely at his own expense (hence the dedication). It was much extended by J.A. Chatwin in 1884/85.

St James' church, Elvetham Road, in 1946. The church was built in 1852 by S.S. Teulon, who also designed Elvetham Hall in Hampshire for the Calthorpe family (hence the road name). The church is currently closed and awaiting a new use.

St Augustine's church, Lyttelton Road, *c.* 1880. It was built in 1868 by J.A. Chatwin (who also rebuilt St Martin's-in-the-Bull-Ring and Aston parish church) on land provided by Joseph Gillott, the pen manufacturer, as part of his plan for the Rotton Park Estate. The tower and spire were added in 1876.

A postcard of St Augustine's (*c.* 1909), with an inset portrait of the then incumbent, Archdeacon Winfrid Burrows (vicar from 1903 to 1912, later Bishop of Truro and then Chichester).

The Baptist Church of the Redeemer, Hagley Road, c. 1890. It was built in 1881/82 by James Cubitt and demolished in the 1970s.

Interior of the Church of the Redeemer, c. 1890. This church was innovative in introducing the modern practice of weekly offerings, in preference to pew rents.

The Oratory, Hagley Road, c. 1890. Originally built by Henry Clutton in around 1852 for Cardinal Newman and his congregation, the Oratory was enlarged in 1858 and 1861 in the Romanesque style by J.H. Pollen. The buildings incorporate the Chapel of St Philip and the former Oratory School, whose pupils included Hilaire Belloc and J.R.R. Tolkien.

The Oratory church, built between 1903 and 1909 by E. Doran Webb as a memorial to Cardinal Newman, has a copper dome and much marble and mosaic work. Essentially Italian Renaissance in style, it contains Corinthian columns from Northern Italy, an altar from a church in Rome, and a seventeenth-century Florentine stoup. This view dates from around 1960.

The south aisle of the Oratory church in 1980, showing on the right some of the Serravezza marble columns shipped from Italy. They were brought to Britain on a steamer two at a time, then hauled by canal barge to Monument Road Wharf.

John Henry Newman (1801-1890) first came to prominence as Vicar of St Mary's, Oxford, and a founding father of the Anglo-Catholic Oxford Movement. The spiritual journey which led him ultimately into the Roman Catholic Church was described in his *Apologia pro vita sua* (1864). A novelist and poet as well as a theologian, Newman was also a pioneer in university education, becoming Rector of the Catholic University of Ireland in 1851. He came to Birmingham in 1849, establishing the present Oratory of St Philip Neri, a community of priests (with adjacent Catholic school), in 1852. He became a Cardinal in 1879. Since his death in 1890, his rooms at the Oratory have remained as he left them.

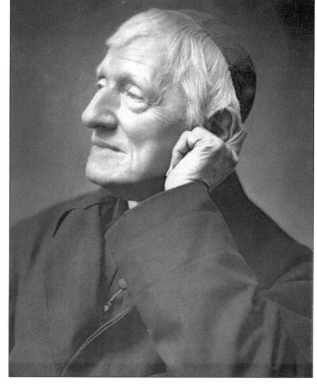

St Germain's church, City Road, was built between 1915 and 1917 by E.F. Reynolds in a brick Romanesque style. It was one of only two churches to be built in England during the First World War and is seen here at the height of the Second World War, in 1942.

The Revd Rolf Gledhill, Vicar of St Germain's from 1939 to 1945, photographed in his study in 1942.

A 1920s view of the church of St Mary and St Ambrose, Pershore Road, which was built in 1897/98 by J.A. Chatwin in the Decorated style, in bright red brick and terracotta.

The Penryn Convent (House of Retreats) on Somerset Road, *c.* 1920.

Five

Health and Education

George Dixon Grammar School, City Road, shortly after opening in 1906.

Founded by the pen manufacturer Sir Josiah Mason in 1875, the University of Birmingham received its Charter in 1900, followed by Lord Calthorpe's offer of land in Edgbaston. The Byzantine designs of Sir Aston Webb (who also designed the Victoria Law Courts) were accepted in 1902, the new building being erected between 1903 and 1909. This view from 1908 shows the construction nearing completion.

The steeply sloping site necessitated terracing on the Bristol Road side; this was all done manually. In the background can be seen the partially completed clock tower, again in 1908. The tower was built from the inside – without scaffolding up to balcony level – and was to rise ultimately to 325ft. Known as 'Joe' – after the first Chancellor, Joseph Chamberlain, whose idea it was – it was modelled on the Mangia Tower in Siena.

ALDERMAN C.G. BEALE   THE RIGHT HON. J. CHAMBERLAIN   SIR OLIVER LODGE

CHANCELLOR OF THE UNIVERSITY.

VICE CHANCELLOR OF
THE UNIVERSITY

PRINCIPAL OF THE
UNIVERSITY.

BIRMINGHAM UNIVERSITY OPENED JULY 7TH BY
THEIR MAJESTIES KING EDWARD VII & QUEEN ALEXANDRA

A postcard commemorating the official opening of the University by King Edward VII on 7 July 1909. Joseph Chamberlain, a long-standing campaigner for the new University, was elected its first Chancellor in 1900, and Sir Oliver Lodge its first Principal. (The Vice-Chancellor's role at this time was largely ceremonial.)

The new University buildings shortly after completion in 1909. The original architect's plans were never completed, and in spite of further building phases from 1926 to 1940 and 1948 to 1957, it was not until the early 1960s that Sir Hugh Casson and Neville Conder were able to create a dignified and spacious campus.

Students' workroom, 1908. Although the scientific and technical departments moved to Edgbaston at this time, the Arts Faculty remained at Mason College in the city centre until 1961.

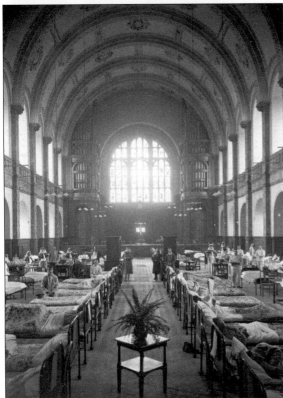

From 1914 – when this picture of the Great Hall was taken – the University buildings were occupied by the 1st Southern General Hospital, which in the course of the First World War treated 125,000 wounded soldiers.

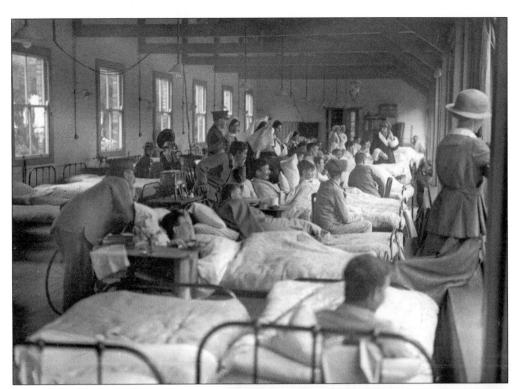

Wounded soldiers watching a production of *Twelfth Night* by the Birmingham Repertory Company, 1914.

University House – seen here with nurses in wartime occupation, *c.* 1914 – was built in 1908, with Neville Chamberlain as the chief fund-raiser. It was the first university hostel for women, and the first to admit male guests. Its first Warden was Margery Fry, a member of the Quaker chocolate family, who subsequently became well known as a penal reformer, Principal of Somerville College, Oxford, and governor of the BBC.

Sir Oliver Lodge, the University's first Principal, passing through the Bristol Road entrance gate, *c.* 1914.

Guild of Undergraduates Committee, 1919/20.

Chancellor's Hall, Augustus Road, in 1930. Formerly a private house, Chancellor's Hall was founded in 1922 to provide for male students at the University some of the social amenities of the older resident universities, and to bring together members of the various faculties. Major extensions were opened in 1927 by Stanley Baldwin, himself a former student at the old Mason College.

The old entrance hall at Chancellor's Hall, 1930. At this time, the cost of residence per term ranged from £21 to £28 17s 6d. The Hall was closed and demolished in the mid-1960s as part of the general redevelopment of Augustus Road.

Francis Brett Young receiving an honorary degree from the then Chancellor Sir Anthony Eden (later Lord Avon) at a special Jubilee ceremony in 1950. Francis Brett Young (1884-1954) was born in Halesowen, and qualified as a doctor at Birmingham Medical School in 1906. He lived for a time on Harborne Road, Edgbaston (which appears as 'Alvaston' in his novel *White Ladies*), and wrote extensively of the Midlands in his thirty novels, which were very popular in the 1930s.

The Barber Institute, the University Art Gallery, was founded in 1932 by Lady Barber in memory of her husband, Sir William Henry Barber, a local solicitor and property developer. It contains a fine collection of European painting and sculpture, as well as an art library and concert hall. To the left of the picture is the eighteenth-century equestrian statue of George I, brought back from Dublin by the Institute's first Director, Professor Thomas Bodkin. This picture was taken in 1975.

The Vale, Edgbaston Park Road, gave its name to the landscaped site now occupied by several halls of residence. It is seen here before the University developments, around 1890.

The Vale – the site of several demolished mansions – owes much to the original Victorian landscaping, although in the 1960s the grounds were modified to accommodate several halls of residence, as depicted here in the 1970s. An attractive artificial lake was created, fed by a natural stream.

Since the foundation of a 'free grammar school' in Birmingham in 1552, King Edward's had passed through several incarnations on New Street, culminating in Sir Charles Barry's Victorian Gothic building. The decision was made to move to a more spacious site in Edgbaston in 1935; the school occupied these temporary wooden buildings for three years until their new premises were completed.

King Edward's School from the playing fields, 1975. The modern building – like its neighbour, King Edward's High School – was designed by Holland Hobbiss. Both schools (which had previously been neighbours in New Street) moved to their new sites in 1940, and maintain close links academically and socially.

The entrance drive to King Edward's, 1977. The present building incorporates a Gothic corridor from New Street now used as the school chapel. Famous old boys include Sir Edward Burne-Jones, H.V. Morton, J.R.R. Tolkien, Godfrey Winn, Enoch Powell, Kenneth Tynan, David Rudkin, Richard Wattis, David Munrow, and Maurice Shock.

George Dixon Grammar School, City Road, seen here in the 1950s, was opened in 1906, replacing the George Dixon Higher Grade School in Oozells Street. It was named after George Dixon (1820-1898), Liberal MP for Edgbaston, who lived on Augustus Road and was a pioneer of state education, helping to found the National Education League in 1869.

King Edward's School, Five Ways, looking down Hagley Road, *c.* 1895. Opened first in 1838 as Birmingham and Edgbaston Proprietary School, it was purchased by the King Edward Foundation in 1882. The school transferred to a more spacious site at Bartley Green in 1958, and the old buildings were later demolished as part of the general redevelopment of the Five Ways area.

Harborne Hill House, site of the future Blue Coat School, at the time of its purchase, 1913. The school had been established on Colmore Row in 1724 'for the purpose of maintaining poor children, teaching them to read and write, and instructing them in the knowledge of the Christian religion'. The intervention of the war in fact delayed the new building until 1930.

Boys of the Blue Coat School, 1910. The school uniform was still at this time a modified form of the eighteenth-century original. From left to right: John Hough, Wilfred Brown, Ernest Tofield, Wilfred Bloor, Tom Chapman, William Herbert, Bernard Hack, Arthur Hancox, Joseph Hinsley, Clinton Tye, Leslie Stone, Reginald Hobby.

Blue Coat School girls glee singing, 1910. From left to right: Alice Cole, Jessie Myatt, Dorothy Langston, Mary Hack, Ada Hooper, Ellen Parsons, Dora Frobisher, Lily Britt, Elsie Flemming, Olive Swindon, Florence Hands.

The School President, Sir Benjamin Stone, who took this photograph, gave a party on the new site on 19 August 1913. Long before the completion of the new building, the land was being used regularly by the school for sporting and recreational purposes, the children walking in a crocodile from town and back again on most occasions.

The new Blue Coat School building, seen here around 1940, was built in 1930 by J.F. Ball and H.W. Simister in a collegiate style consisting of several detached blocks arranged round three sides of a large grassy quadrangle. The statues, set in niches, of a boy and girl wearing the traditional school uniform are copies of the originals (housed inside) which once adorned the façade at Colmore Row. In 1960, in acknowledgement of changing needs, the school became an independent boarding and day preparatory school, with thirty Foundation scholars.

The Royal Institution for the Blind, on Carpenter Road, was built in 1851/52 in the Jacobean style by Samuel Hemming. It rapidly acquired a good reputation for caring and innovative education, training over 600 students annually by 1900, expanding on to a site in Harborne, and later acquiring Lickey Grange, former home of Lord Austin. In 1953, the Carpenter Road building became the BBC Midland Headquarters, but was demolished following the BBC's move to Pebble Mill in the late 1960s.

Pupils at play at the Royal Institution for the Blind, c. 1900.

Blind pupils at work, c. 1900. Among several valuable innovations, the school invented a system of embossed shorthand, with an accompanying typing machine.

The Royal Institution for the Instruction of Deaf and Dumb Children, on Church Road, was opened in 1814 by Gabriel Jean Marie De Lys, a refugee from the French Revolution and a leading physician at the General Hospital. The main buildings were erected in the 1850s. By 1900, when this picture was taken, the school was teaching 175 children, being described as 'in everything up-to-date, and one of the most complete Deaf and Dumb Schools in the kingdom'.

Classes at the Deaf and Dumb Institution, 1900. The school continued until 1984, the premises now being occupied by the Princess Royal Centre (National Deaf-Blind and Rubella Association).

Edgbaston Church of England College for Girls, on Calthorpe Road, was founded in 1886 by Dr Charles Gore (later first Bishop of Birmingham) and a number of other influential clergymen who were concerned by what they felt to be the very secular outlook of many girls' schools at the time. The fine Georgian house which still forms the core of the school was considered a 'favoured spot sufficiently far from the noise of steam trams to be suitable'. This picture dates from 1897.

Parents' Day at the College, c. 1900. In common with most schools in Edgbaston, there are extensive park-like grounds. A strong Anglican tradition is maintained, with close links to St George's church across the road.

A college class in around 1900. From September 1999 the school will be co-educational.

Penryn, on Somerset Road, was originally built as a private residence by John Henry Chamberlain, later becoming a convent and then a Catholic school for boys. It is seen here in 1896.

The First XI football team at Penryn School, 1929-30.

The cricket team at Penryn, c. 1930.

An aerial view of the Queen Elizabeth Hospital taken in 1952, showing its then still spacious and open setting. Opened in 1938, and incorporating the University Medical School (the long, low façade to the left), it rapidly became one of Britain's leading teaching hospitals. Since this picture was taken, the site has been intensively developed with many new departments, although the future of the original buildings is currently under discussion.

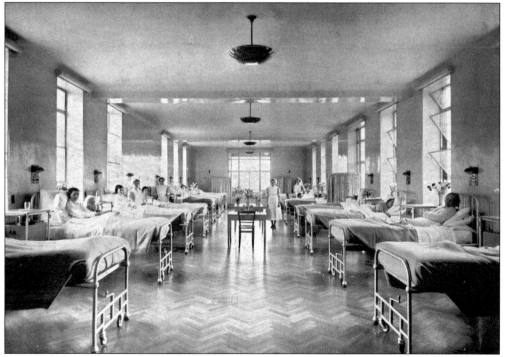

A ward in the new hospital, shortly after completion, in 1939.

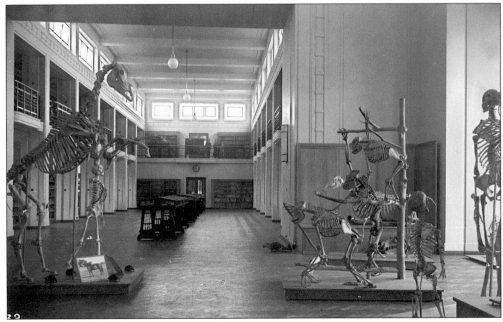

The Medical School Museum, 1939.

Sister's sitting room in the Queen Elizabeth Hospital, 1939.

Six
Parks and Gardens

Cannon Hill Park, c. 1930.

Louisa Anne Ryland (1814-1889), daughter of a wealthy landowner, was born at The Laurels, Hagley Road, Edgbaston, though the family later moved to Barford Hill in Warwick, where she remained until her death. She devoted her life to charitable works, providing the village of Sherbourne with a new church, helping to restore Aston Hall, and giving generously to Birmingham General Hospital, the Midland Institute and the School of Art. Her best known gifts to Birmingham are, however, Cannon Hill Park and Victoria Park, Small Heath. Miss Ryland donated the land and paid for the layout in each case.

The bandstand at Cannon Hill Park, c. 1900. The park was opened on 1 September 1873, with a minimum of formality, the Mayor and a few councillors merely being present as the gates were flung open and a card of welcome from Louisa Ryland was handed to each person who passed through.

The boating lake at Cannon Hill Park, *c.* 1900. Two large lakes, as well as a bathing pool and smaller ponds, formed part of the original gift.

The boating lake, 1974.

Feeding the ducks at Cannon Hill Park, *c.* 1900.

Feeding the ducks in the 1970s.

The South African War Memorial in Cannon Hill Park, *c.* 1900.

The River Rea in flood, 1931. Birmingham's river has always been easily accessible in the Cannon Hill area, and the recent development of the Rea Valley Walkway has provided several miles of attractive riverside walks.

The Golden Lion, Digbeth, 1887. In an early example of conservation work, this sixteenth-century inn was dismantled and re-erected at Cannon Hill Park in 1911.

The Golden Lion at Cannon Hill Park, 1931. Originally used as a summer pavilion, it is currently closed and awaiting a new use.

A characteristic 'Dutch' scene at the Tulip Festival, Cannon Hill Park, 1968. Very popular throughout the 1960s and 1970s, the Tulip Festival began as an Anglo-Dutch venture, later expanding into the International Spring Festival and including the participation of local community groups. In the festival's heyday, thirty-three different countries took part, highlights including a balloon race, free-fall parachuting, a veteran car rally, military bands, folk dancing, pizza and pasta bars, beer gardens, open-air art exhibitions and craft stalls.

Folk dancing at the Tulip Festival, 1970.

Crowds attending the Tulip Festival in the 1970s.

Since the war, Cannon Hill Park has considerably developed its facilities for large-scale entertainment. The open-air theatre adjacent to the Midlands Arts Centre for Young People (later MAC) was particularly popular during the 1960s and 1970s. Here a dramatic performance is in progress during the summer of 1969.

A beekeeper at Birmingham Nature Centre, adjoining Cannon Hill Park, in 1978. Opened in 1975 on the site of the former Birmingham Zoo, the centre occupies $6\frac{1}{2}$ acres of attractive wooded grounds at the confluence of the River Rea and the Bourn Brook. As far as possible, the 134 species of British and European wildlife are housed in naturalistic settings, the aim being to give city dwellers – especially children – some understanding of nature and the countryside.

Calthorpe Park was laid out on land offered by Lord Calthorpe in 1856 and officially opened by
the Duke of Cambridge on 1 June 1857. It lies between the River Rea and Pershore Road, on
the Balsall Heath/Edgbaston border. In this photograph from around 1916, the spire of St Mary
and St Ambrose can be seen rising in the background.

Children playing in Calthorpe Park, 1970.

The Vale in the 1970s, looking towards the University across the artificial lake created in the 1960s. The park, which accommodates University halls of residence, is formed from the grounds of three vanished mansions – Wyddrington, Maple Bank, and The Vale.

Children playing by the bridge at Edgbaston Reservoir, 1906.

Walking beside Edgbaston Reservoir, with the spire of St Augustine's rising in the background, 1968. Situated off Rotton Park Road, the Reservoir was planned by Thomas Telford between 1825 and 1827 as a feeder for the Birmingham Canal. A notable wildlife centre, it is now an important recreational resource, particularly popular with yachtsmen, fishermen, walkers and joggers.

The reservoir during the Great Drought of 1976.

Edgbaston Reservoir at dusk in the 1970s.

Below opposite: The fountain and glasshouse at the Botanical Gardens, *c.* 1875. The site – at Holly Farm, Edgbaston – was leased from Lord Calthorpe, and the gardens laid out in 1831/32 to the designs of John Claudius Loudon (1783-1843), the noted landscape gardener and architect. His wife Jane was a native of Bartley Green, Birmingham, and later became a famous writer on gardening in her own right.

The entrance to the Botanical Gardens, *c.* 1906. Birmingham Botanical and Horticultural Society was founded in 1829, its aims being to form a comprehensive collection of plants (especially recent foreign imports), to advance botanical knowledge, and encourage a love of gardening. The gardens are unique in that they are the only provincial botanical gardens from that period that are still owned and administered by a private society.

The fountain in around 1900. It was designed by Charles Edge and installed in 1850, but was for some years filled in and used for floral displays. It was fully restored in 1982 to commemorate the 150th anniversary of the gardens.

One of a series of panoramic views of the Botanical Gardens taken in 1906/07 by Thomas Humphreys, who was Curator from 1903 to 1932.

The Main Lawn sloping down from the glasshouses – seen here in Thomas Humphreys' view of around 1906 – has remained a constant feature of the Botanical Gardens since their inception.

Another Humphreys view of the Main Lawn, looking towards the bandstand, again *c*. 1906. Although beginning as private subscription grounds, the Botanical Gardens admitted school parties almost from the start, and from October 1844 working-class visitors were welcomed on Mondays and Tuesdays on payment of a penny per person – an important concession when there were no local public parks.

The terrace and glasshouses at the Botanical Gardens, c. 1950. The glasshouses – partly reconstructed in recent years – were built by Henry Hope and Sons in 1884/85.

The Main Lawn at the Gardens, c. 1950.

Visitors watching the monkeys, *c*. 1950. From 1910 to 1960, the Gardens maintained a large zoological collection, including llamas, chimpanzees, wallabies, goats, sheep, a mongoose, a laughing jackass, a coatimundi and bears. More recently, the emphasis has been on exotic birds rather than animals (with indoor and outdoor aviaries), and an extensive waterfowl enclosure.

California Brickworks outing, 1906.

A wedding group with the Palm House in the background, 1934. For the past century, private functions have been a prominent feature of the Botanical Gardens and an important source of income.

Tennis at the Botanical Gardens, *c.* 1906. As early as 1835 an archery and croquet lawn had been set out; but from 1868 a portion of the lower grounds was sublet to the Edgbaston Archery and Lawn Tennis Society.

Seven
Leisure and Sport

A yacht race at Edgbaston Reservoir, *c.* 1910.

Australia *v*. Warwickshire at the County Cricket Ground, Edgbaston, 1899. Founded in 1882 and initially using Aston Lower Grounds, Warwickshire County Cricket Club was offered some 'rough grazing land' by Lord Calthorpe in 1885. The new ground was originally shared with tennis, bowls, lacrosse, football and baseball. The first cricket match was a two-day contest on 7-8 June 1886 (a draw between WCC and MCC), watched by 3,000 people.

Warwickshire County Cricket Club pavilion, *c.* 1895. The club achieved first-class status in 1894, with a trio of conclusive wins – *v.* Nottinghamshire at Trent Bridge (by 6 wkts), *v.* Surrey at the Oval (by 7 wkts), and *v.* Kent at home (by 8 wkts).

A hockey match at the County Cricket Ground, 1903.

Fairlight on Ampton Road, *c.* 1947. Eighty years previously this was the home of Mr J.B.A. Perera, a merchant, who staged the first game of lawn tennis in around 1865, between Mr Perera and his friend Major Gem, a well-known local sportsman and clubman. The two men afterwards moved to Leamington, where in 1872 they helped found the world's first tennis club, which played in the grounds of the Manor House Hotel. Major Gem compiled a list of rules.

Edgbaston Archery and Lawn Tennis Society was founded in 1860 (twelve years earlier than the Leamington club), but concentrated initially on archery and croquet, taking up lawn tennis around 1874. Their sports ground originally formed part of the Botanical Gardens but was sublet by the Gardens Committee from 1868. The match shown here took place in 1898.

A Priory Tennis Club match (Dorothy Round *v.* Señora Lizana), 1937. Starting in 1875/76 with two grass courts in a field off Bristol Road, the club was one of the first to be founded solely for the playing of lawn tennis, later moving to the site of a medieval priory on Sir Harry's Road, where there was steady expansion from the original four grass courts. It is now the scene of international tournaments.

Winter sports on the frozen lake at Cannon Hill Park, 1961.

The Midlands Arts Centre (MAC) in the 1970s. The centre began at Cannon Hill Park in the early 1960s as the Midlands Arts Centre for Young People. The site expanded gradually as funds became available and now appeals widely to a family audience, with theatres, cinema, music and dance studios, art galleries, a bookshop and extensive catering facilities. The bar and courtyard are the scene of arts performances of many kinds, while the Centre hosts book and craft fairs, the annual Birmingham Film and TV Festival, and the Readers' and Writers' Festival.

The audience at the Midlands Arts Centre's open air theatre in the 1970s.

A vintage car rally at Cannon Hill Park, 1962. The car pictured nearest the camera is a 1903 Sunbeam, made not far away, in Wolverhampton.

Edgbaston Assembly Rooms, *c*. 1890. The Assembly Rooms, on the corner of Francis Road and Hagley Road, Five Ways, were opened in 1884, and were extensively used for meetings, plays, concerts, dances and receptions. The Pilgrim Players, forerunners of the Birmingham Repertory Theatre, used to perform here. From 1937, the Assembly Rooms were used by the Warwickshire Masonic Temple while also maintaining their wider social role. The building was demolished in the late 1960s as part of the Five Ways redevelopment.

The drawing room, Edgbaston Assembly Rooms, *c.* 1890.

The ballroom, Edgbaston Assembly Rooms, *c.* 1890.

The White Swan, Harborne Road, 1933. Edgbaston's oldest pub began around 1700 as a row of cottages, later becoming a coaching inn. Reputedly haunted by the ghost of John Wentworth, who shot himself following the death of his mistress on Harborne Hill, it retains the air of a country inn in spite of several post-war renovations.

Visitors to the Plough and Harrow with their tiller-steered car. The car is primitive, with solid tyres, and probably dates from around 1900. The picture was taken after December 1903, when car registration plates were introduced; this vehicle was registered in London.

Below opposite: The Plough and Harrow on Hagley Road is Edgbaston's oldest hotel, tracing its history back to at least 1612, though the present building is early Victorian. While fully modernized internally, its exterior remains remarkably unchanged, retaining the air of a country house. It is seen here in around 1890.

A holiday scene outside the Tower Ballroom, beside Edgbaston Reservoir, in 1968. The ballroom was previously a roller-skating rink.

Fishermen at Edgbaston Reservoir in the 1970s.